Sweet to Burn

Beverly Burch

Arlington, Virginia

SWEET TO BURN. Copyright © 2004 by Beverly Burch

All rights reserved under International and Pan-American Copyright Conventions.
Printed in the United States of America.

With the exception of brief quotations in the body of critical articles or reviews, no part of this book may be reproduced or transmitted in any form or by any means, graphic, electronic, or mechanical, including photocopying, recording, taping, or by any information storage or retrieval system, without the permission in writing from the publisher.

Published by Gival Press, an imprint of Gival Press, LLC.
For information please write:
Gival Press, LLC, P. O. Box 3812, Arlington, VA 22203.
Website: www.givalpress.com

First edition ISBN 1-928589-23-5
Library of Congress Control Number: 2004111774

Cover art: "Red Canna with Water Drops" Copyright © 2004 by Birgit O'Connor.
Author photo by Linda O'Brien.
Format and design by Ken Schellenberg.

Advance Praise for *Sweet to Burn*

"Novelistic in scope, but packing the emotional intensity of lyric poetry, Beverly Burch's *Sweet to Burn* charts the relationship of two distinct and dissimilar spirits who test the boundaries of love and trust over a lifetime. The strength of the narrative is matched by the richness of the individual poems. Indeed, these poems pass the ultimate test—each one can stand alone as an exquisite example of mature craft. Who thought you could say about a book of poetry—'I couldn't put it down!'?"

—Eloise Klein Healy, *Passing*

"*Sweet to Burn* tells the story of two women who meet and make a life together. They contend with families—the ones they came from, and the new one they create with an adopted daughter. They contend, too, with loss and desire in the context of long love. In starkly realistic and lyrical poems, Beverly Burch explores that love with all of its attendant doubts and unexpected moments of grace."

—Kim Addonizio, *What Is This Thing Called Love*

"'The subject of this story is desire.' *Sweet to Burn* combines daring lyric intensity—stars that 'swung like a roulette wheel,' a kingfisher 'stricken with infinity'—with the richness and depth of the love story. Beverly Burch knows how to skate the razor's edge between action and image so each hones the other: 'it wasn't her gold chain but how it fell / across her throat.' These poems confront the 'impossibility' and delicious necessity of love that 'wounds like that splinter of bone hidden in the hot curry.'"

—Robert Thomas, *Door to Door*

"Beverly Burch is a master at exploring the subtle seasons of relationships, both the heartaches and the joys. Her imagery is fresh and accessible—the message undeniably rich and moving. Fabulous lines from *Sweet to Burn* will stay with you longer after you've closed the book. As a poet, Burch has a poignant and powerful voice that will no doubt leave its mark on the world of poetry. I highly recommend this portal to a remarkable soul."

—Janet I. Buck, *Tickets to a Closing Play*

Also by Beverly Burch

On Intimate Terms

Other Women

Grateful acknowledgment is made to the following journals where these poems first appeared, sometimes in an earlier form.

"Conjunction" and "Sunday Hike at Point Reyes" in *anteup*.
"After Midnight 1 & 2" and "Evening Inversions" in *Borderlands*.
"It's Her Body She Misses Now" in *Calyx*.
"Beatitude" in *Coracle*.
"After We Fight" in *Comstock Review*, reprinted in *Calyx*.
"Old Sweethearts" in *Disquieting Muses (DMQ Review)*.
"TEN to TEN" in *Lullwater Review*.
"Perimenopausal Lovers Sleeping in Mid-Winter" in *Many Mountains Moving*.
"Teenager on the Half-shell" in *North American Review*.
"Insomnia" in *Peralta Press*.
"Sky/Branches/Sky" in *Poetry International*.
"In Her Absence" and "Kayaking Close to Shore" on *poetrymagazine.com*.
"At the Volcano" and "Damage" in *Red Rock Review*.
"Dead Center" in *River City*.
"Tang and Hue" and "This Way or That" in *Slant*.
"Not Easy to Know" and "Not a Marriage" in *Santa Clara Review*.
"Hard Rain in San Francisco" in *Spillway*.
"Above the Bay" in *Tar River Poetry*.

Thanks to Kim Addonizio, Cyrus Cassells, Stephen Dunn, Carol Jenkins, Diane Kirsten-Martin, Linda O'Brien, Joan Hamerman Robbins, Bill Robbins, Richard Silberg and Robert Thomas for reading and consultation on all or parts of this ms. in various stages of its evolution. Thanks also to the members of Thirteen Ways and Word of Mouth poetry groups for their skill in balancing support with that sensitive business of criticism.

Contents

I — First Sight 15
    Play Back 16
    Wind Shear 17
    Mid-morning, Briones Valley 18
    Talk After Midnight 1 19
    After Midnight 2 21
    Not a Marriage 22
    Tang and Hue 23

II — Chosen 25
    Labor and Delivery 26
    Conjunction 27
    Jeopardy 28
    Ordinary Life 29
    Five A.M., Two Years Old 30
    Doppelganger 31
    All-You-Can-Eat Shrimp 32

III — Only Human 33
    Promises 34
    Driving to Zion 35
    Sky/Branches/Sky 36
    Above the Bay 37
    Kayaking Close to Shore 38
    Just Look 39
    Sunday Hike at Point Reyes 40
    Solomon's Child 41
    Early Dawn Parallax 42
    Urgent Care 43

IV — The Family Circle 45
    The Laws of Planetary Motion 46
    This Way or That 47
    Ten to Ten 48
    Eating at the In-laws 49
    The View from the North Coast 51
    What We Told Ourselves 52
    At the Volcano 53
    In Her Absence 54

    Return 55

V — Perimenopausal Lovers Sleeping in Mid-winter 57
    Late Season Mothers 58
    Star Quality 59
    Kissing 60
    Hard Rain in San Francisco 61
    Displeased 62
    Insomnia 63
    Teenager on the Half-Shell 64
    Exposure 65
    Another Black December 66
    Winter Storm, Mendocino 67
    A Sleep Genius 68
    Evening Inversions 69
    Damage 70
    After We Fight 71

Vll — The Afternoon Nap 73
    Beatitude 74
    It's Her Body I Miss Now 76
    Not Easy to Know 77
    Edisto Island 78
    Dead Center 79

Vll — From the Backyard at Nine P. M. 81
    Out of the Ordinary 82
    Painted Moon, Painted Valley 83
    Appetite 84
    Lost Cause 85
    Four A. M. at the Open Window 86
    Cutting Edge 87
    Unseasoned 88
    Exposure 89
    A New Period of Red 90
    Old Sweethearts 91

Sweet to Burn

ride joy until
it cracks like an egg
—Rita Dove, *Thomas and Beulah*

The Subject of This Story Is Desire

Isn't that the subject of every story? Desire, how it steals, careless where it leaves things, who it orphans. Lovers going under, children falling in its wake so desire can fill its glowing hunger. Doesn't it tumble everyone? Even animals. Look—the spider quivers in her web as the fly passes, the hawk swoons above the meadow of its last mouse. And plants, the lily toils not nor spins, still it reaches for the sun, hour after hour.

A breeze stirs branches of the plum tree, petals drift across the sidewalk—soon the ichor of longing rises in your throat. But why name what's ordinary as air? Necessity, how the voice unblocks the windpipe, even sputtering. How desire gives way, pinned to the butterfly board—a winged artifact spread out for admiration, our desirous study.

I — First Sight

A woman walks into a bar, a lesbian bar in San Francisco. She's all alone, feels like a handful of loose change. In fact she places two quarters on the bar, circles them around each other while she studies the bartender. She's good at seduction. Soon the bartender serves her a Dubonnet on the house, asks her name. Her name is Alice.

Four women walk into the bar, choose a table in the corner. They look alike, lots of dark curly hair. You'd be confused whether they're paired—see how they sit close, talk low, touch each other and the hands linger. Maybe they're all lovers, ménage à quatre. *Or the kind of friends who act like lovers, never sleep together. One is named Meg.*

Alice and Meg catch each other's eye, but Meg turns away. Alice asks Meg to dance and Meg's too surprised to hesitate. Alice meets Meg's smile—clear as plate glass, no distortion, no guile at all—and her hands tremble touching the small of Meg's back.

Play Back

Alice

    Weeks after, I imagine her a stranger again,
    want the jolt of meeting one more time.
    Outside, after the bar, stars swung
    like a roulette wheel. In the stiff breeze
    streets were almost soundless.
    Movements of her body, her hands
    in the air, reached me like tiny shock waves.
    She didn't feel this, checked her watch,
    worried what the friends would think.

    I had to turn away, too much showed in my face.

    I knew her already, some left-behind dream:
    it wasn't her gold chain but how it fell
    across her throat. Not her green sweater
    but how it rose from her waist. Not her long legs
    but the way they crossed as she stood.
    Not the vein of red in her hair but the heat
    it gave off. Not the suede boots, but their rhythm
    on the sidewalk as she went back for her things.

Wind Shear

Meg

Watching her at the bar I thought I'd draw
her face—shaped like a heart—
the curve of her throat, that slender jaw.
Then there she was, at my table.

Three nights we didn't part.
She took me to the river. We swam naked
in water too dark and green to see our bodies.
Then Mt. Diablo—she likes to drive,
fast and often. She roasted chilis,
cooked empanadas over hot coals.
Her pursuit, a wind at my back.

I let the phone ring, see friends, paint
every morning. She has to wait.
I send a card copied from a French landscape:
pale colors, soft shrubs, hillside,
two women waking up under the sun:
one wide-eyed, one slowly starting to stretch.

Mid-morning, Briones Valley

Meg

Violet-green swallows loop over grassland:
in the blue air they look like fish
whirling in swift current. Birds must live
for summer—hot-bodied insects,
air that expands all morning as mercury rises.

Alice and I climb a crescent-shaped ridge,
breathe eucalyptus, heated earth,
dry grass. She liked my card,
insisted on its likeness here: pale green
chapparal, purpled branches against yellow hills,
slopes mounded, smoothed
like clay in human hands.
Native grass grows thick beside the trail,
the same yellow-green, streaked with purple.

I'm yielding, I feel it.
We're driving home, sudden rain speckles
the window. These days together,
beads of water on glass, not a pattern,
a refraction. They're altering the light.

Talk After Midnight 1

Alice: Never Fixed

I remember South Carolina like a first lover,
    cruelties confused with attractions: languid Sea Islands,
        low-country roads, palmetto, crape myrtle.
    Heat blanketed the prospect of anything changing.

Summer days I cycled from Charleston after new territory,
    came back by noon when humidity, haze weakened ambition,
        then circled genteel lushness of fine neighborhoods,
    pastel houses, piazzas on the side.

My father worked the boatyards,
    a sometime-shrimper away for weeks.
        When the screen door slammed just before dinner
            and his rolling gait lumbered toward the kitchen,
    we knew he was drunk already.

My brothers and I scattered like peas.
    Mother fed us on the back porch,
        left us out till lightning bugs lifted to the pines,
    the moon trapped in tall branches.
        We'd tiptoe in, listen for his snoring.

I learned to love the dark, its damp coolness,
    the way our meager world disappeared,
        scent of gardenias drifting through the night.

Lying in grass, I picked my way across the sky,
    oriented like a mariner: over there—India,
        down there—Argentina.

Ocean air was second-skin, a steamy coat I wore all summer.
    I cycled remote beaches for the tang of low-tide,
        slap of cold in December.

And horizon, the Atlantic pinned against the sky, yet never fixed.
    Stormy or still, the rolling, loose horizon.

The summer I graduated, my father ran off the road, drunk.
    My mother, who'd needed little, took the insurance,
        travelled for the first time:
    Malayasia, Thailand on a freight steamer.

I short-cut college to see how far I'd get on my own.
    Only my brother, always beyond me, stuck fast,
        kept rooms ready for our return.

After Midnight 2

Meg: Good Soldier

At eight a record storm swept Mankota.
I shoveled our long driveway
for the salute on my father's face.

Life in Minnesota was not enchanting, not disturbing.
Cold prairie, eternal whiteness of snow and ice,
taught necessity, numbness, keeping close
to whatever warmed you.

Mother a math teacher, father a high school principal.
Childhood meant cousins, catechisms, the annual class fair.

Art school, California, my stroke of independence—
mother hated it, my father finally applauded.
I might have stayed in the cold, married,
but San Francisco changed me. It's that simple.

I love what's on the surface—color, shape,
the feel of things. A ripe mango: how its curve
fits the palm of my hand.
Smooth skim of a newly-paved street, glide of a bicycle.
Even the shine of hardwood floors as I clean.

You want more.
To get beneath things, reach the rich heart.
I fear this urge—maybe I have no interior, am mostly skin.
Not a mango, but one of those strange oranges:
thick, thick peel,
a hard pulpy little knot within.

Not a Marriage

Meg

But a close resemblance.
Four months after we meet, we sign a lease
on Potrero Hill. Lacking furniture, Alice
puts something of hers in each room:
coiled grass baskets from Charleston beneath
my watercolors, her grandmother's quilt
on my brass bed. Alice unpacks
the first day. I set up a studio:
sturdy slanted table, stacks
of porous paper with ragged edges,
shelf with a precise rainbow of colored tubes.

We open a joint account—printed checks
the only public papers with both our names.
Drink wine on the deck at night,
oblivious to the rattle of cars
straining up the street. Bundled in jackets
when fog moves in, we talk
long-term plans, spin the future before us:
delicate web, airy trellis
to catch us up, hold us together
in the absence of ceremony, lawful bonds.

Tang and Hue

Alice

A dream job: I'm learning pastry
at a bakery in the Castro. My hands work
glossy clumps of butter into mounds of flour,
stay deep in pillowy dough all morning.
I test for doneness, taste for the tang
of lemon, burnt sweetness of almond.

The afternoon I visit Meg's classroom
students streak huge sections of cardboard
with blobby continents in orange, purple, green
on an opaque ocean of blue.
Others' hands, gummy with paste, fix
national flags, children's photos on finished pieces.

Meg's the epicenter—
I hardly see her for the ripple of girls
expanding around her. To get through to Meg—
everyone wants that.

At home, she puts *Tosca* on the stereo
and I cook: braised eggplant and tomatoes,
baby squash browned in olive oil with bread crumbs.
I set plates on the table, see my mother's
fingers handling the cutlery.
I tell Meg: women marry for this—
the bright kitchen, copper pans on the walls,
an amber-lit dinner.

Scent of the past all over the present, you go
rapt as a hound into tomorrow.

11 — Chosen

In line at the bank a woman nuzzles a baby in a sling. Alice starts to weep. She wants to tumble on the floor with this baby, rock its curled body through a long night. Too close to 35, she's got the ache. The blitz of falling, pull of Meg's elusiveness—it's waned. Make life like a string of lights, Alice says. If you hit a blank space, seek another flare.

Meg says: We're happy like this. Too soon. A child needs a father. It's artificial. *Alice falls into a blue fright—what if Meg won't change? Six months. A year. Meg relents:* What about adoption?

March, April, nothing but paperwork, laying bets. Impossible—the careless universe dropping a child into their arms. Mid-September, still no word. Alice lies awake, hating Meg, her heartless sleeping. Then a teenage girl in Texas picks their picture from the pile: the two of them on their deck, Meg's arms around Alice. They're the ones, *she says.*

Labor and Delivery

Meg

A three a.m. phone call, a hurried flight,
two days, one night, pacing
hospital corridors, hardly an hour spent
at the cheap room we rented.
Off to the social worker—*Didn't know
you were ga-ay*, in that slow Texas way—
then the lawyer, and racing
back to the ward—a girl, dark hair, dark eyes.
In the hall we name her: Talia.
A nurse shifts back and forth with the baby—
two *women claim her?*
Lifted off at last, Dallas to San Francisco,
Alice cradles the baby, I hum tired lullabyes.
A flight attendant brings a bottle
of champagne from first class,
wraps up another,
intrigued with our journey,
the tiny child, two sleepy mothers.
Sailing through that monochrome
blue over Tahoe, Alice turns weepy.
Talia's wailing, but we've crossed
into California, close enough to feel home.

Conjunction

Meg

Both of us mother to the same child,
trying to occupy the same cubic
meters of space, displace the same atoms

in the physics of the family. Each primary—
an indivisible figure cleaved
in two. Alice can't stop reaching

for the baby in my arms. We answer
in tandem when Talia cries.
Lean over the crib bar in unison—

a mythical creature, the two-headed mother.
Suffering love's wounds at the same moment,
daily invading the other's territory.

Like blind objects that collide in the dark,
we discover we're both right there.
Ah, well. We wanted to be that close.

Jeopardy

Alice

This child is mine. I lifted her first,
touched her skin. Bones of my arms, skin
of my fingers still feel that. Her first smile, my own jaw
eased, my ribs heaved open.

At bedtime when she wails—
great down-mouthed despair of a cartoon character—
I rock her in the dark and my elbows,
blades of my back curl with her.

I snatch her from the sandpile
before she pockets a dirty fist in plump cheeks—
my spine bends instantly, my legs quick
because they know.

I hoard each day
the way a woman dying would—even as I crave
to step out the door, drive off alone
down some blue highway.

Up early with Talia
I head to the marina, walk until she sleeps
in her stroller. Dawn glitters across the water.
I move my thoughts on

to what's to be done today. How often
I do that. As if the tug of Earth's beauty
is lethal, could lodge like an hook,
jerking my breath clean away.

Ordinary Life

Meg

There's jasmine trellised on the garage wall,
abutilon hangs small white lanterns
on the fence and red anemones fall open
like deep kisses.

Home, neighborhood,
clean laundry, clean floors, dinner every night.
Even Aunt Ingrid wants to visit.
(Those ties knit back, all I fled.)
An ordinary life, this queer family,
two mothers, a child.

I sketch from photos: fat baby walking
on wobbly legs, cherub napping
in mother's arms.
I wondered why people like such art.
A pleasure, the commonplace:
uncommon it is, if it happens to you.

Five A.M., Two Years Old

Meg

Resolute as cat after mouse,
Talia stalks the hallway.
On the threshold of our room she watches
for a sign—
an opening eye, a sleepy wave-in.
Foot on box spring, knee on mattress,
she hauls herself up, the gap between us.
Her soft flesh shivers, homes in
on the all-night dream.
Burrows, a blind nursling.
Breathes in Alice, rolls over to me.
Nestles like suckling, sweet sustenance
she's never known.
Only animal pleasures of early morning.

Doppelganger

Alice

My double—she goes on and on.
Back to dewy lawns in Charleston whenever she wishes.
Weeks in the Selkirks or walking Waimea Canyon.
While I prune the plum tree, she
explores Anza-Borrego. I read in bed, she sleeps
under stars on Orcas Island.
I call home when I'm late, but my double's
on another long fall, new infatuation.

In dreams I climb white-sheeted mountains
of Bhutan, sail off to the vast glitter of Antarctica.
She grows surly: you chose home and a bed,
said you'd like to turn down lights each night
with the same lover.

All-You-Can-Eat Shrimp

Alice

In that cafe on the coast of my dream
I cook only one food, shrimp.
Tide's coming in, my father's boat visible
on the horizon. I slide peeled shrimp
into a golden scrim of butter. Its flesh
hits the pan with a faint cry.
Translucent shells land in a cracked basin—
empty fingers, my mother's hands
fallen to pieces. I poach shrimp
in wine. Pairs of them curl toward each other
like parting lips. From the backroom
my mother's dark elegy floats in: *Shrimp boats
are a-comin', their sails are in sight.*
Sweaty customers pack into padded booths,
dip pink meat into aioli, lift forks
to their mouths, chew tender morsels.

Garlic infuses the air, lemon
scents my skin as I slice, whisk.
With a good catch, my father will be finishing
a bottle. I scatter chopped cilantro,
shallots, roasted peppers over platters
of broiled shrimp. A bad one, he's on his second.
I crumble bread into fine grains, beat eggs,
coat the bowed meat, plop it in the fryer.
The dark cradle of his boat rocks and rocks.
Oil spits, sizzles. I stir cocktail sauce,
balance shrimp along a bowl's edge the way
my heart hangs on the arc of this dream.

Yesterday, a feast. Now only shrimp,
red-veined, reeking of tidewater. No matter how
I cook it, I begin to hate shrimp.

lll — Only Human

No wonder people go off to caves, try to free themselves from desire. But isn't desire in the cave too? Its rhythm like a heartbeat, it can't let up.

Look at Alice—she holds onto everything: in dreams her first lover comes back, sits down to breakfast again with that same deep sigh, and her mother's there in the tiny flat where she lived alone in Seattle. Or she's sixteen, talking on the phone to her best friend (who was perfect, who stole her boyfriend in the end) but it's a cell phone she's using in that schoolyard of the 60s. As if she could still be young, keep falling in love, and have what she has now—Meg, Talia.

Meg's a believer, she'll do love right. If a fairy tale needs heroic defeats, she'll endure a dragon. But sometimes the happy ending comes too early in the story. And the story goes on.

Cave or no cave, they're caught.

Promises

Meg

Alice speaks of the new cook at her job:
she studied in France, worked at Chez Panisse,
travelled in her twenties, cafe to cafe—
Alice stays at work late, long after lunchtime.
Then suddenly on duty for dinner,
comes home giddy with wine.

One night she disappears, tiptoes in at five a.m.
I stalk off, make it to 24th & Mission
before a trio of drunks bawls something about
some pussy and I catch a cab home.

Alice is in with Talia, who sleeps
in spite of Alice's weeping. She follows me
to our bedroom, tries to hold the hand
I pull away. *I've been torn. I'm relieved you know,*
she says. But I don't know anything.
I can't listen to confession when I have
no absolution to offer.

It won't happen again.
I'll change jobs. We'll take some trips.

Driving to Zion

Alice

Wandering in the desert
for deliverance—the fiery furnace
of Utah's sun, the cloudless blue,
orange pillars of rock—
near Escalante we stop at an overlook.
The silence turns my agitation to ether,
thins it over the landscape.
Nothing to hold onto there.

I remember Talia in Anza-Borrego:
I'd promised the desert would be amazing.
Half an hour into its stark sameness
she asks, *So where's the desert?*
I say, *Here. Right out the window.*
Where? she asks, *Where?*

On a scattered red rock trail I stray
toward the sound of water.
Ten feet ahead a cougar stares. I step back—
fear that's almost envy.
The cat's a solid chunk of animal,
its eyes on me. Then it ambles off.

Yesterday outside of Moab I saw a hawk
skim the mesas, not a feather stirred
by the draft. It hovered, still as God,
focused on the hunt.
If only I could do that.
But I'm not that kind of creature.
My kind keeps driving, wasn't born with a gift
for recognizing what it's after,
even when it's all around me.

Sky/Branches/Sky

Meg

On a low-sloping hillside in early November
somewhere in southern Utah, I lie back after a walk.
Alice goes on about something—
I've stopped listening. We're inside a circle,
tall trunks of bare aspens, cottonwoods, the sky
shot through with dark limbs.
Indigo sky, fan of naked trees—their shapes
cut a pattern for bleak joy.
However alone, I feel the imprint will hold:
sky setting off dark branches, trees
arching on that cold canopy, near-winter.

Above the Bay

Meg

Ohlone Canyon turns slick after heavy rain,
but we agree to go, hope the muck's hardened.
Our trail's churned, congealed, a mosaic—
sticks-rock-mud—a rough ribbon in the woods.

We hold hands inside my pocket. *A truce,*
Alice says. Why does she name it, make us self-
conscious? *Signs of recovery.* Yes.
I could take issue, but the sky's a blue relief,

Farallones visible past the Golden Gate.
Why is tenderness not simple? Like the throb
of warmth in April, dependable the way
spring offers itself. And the glossy body

of the bay below, sun falling across
water, gold paint poured over broken glass.

Kayaking Close to Shore

Alice

Three times the call of the kingfisher
rattles over us as it veers from the forest,
suspends itself mid-air like a creature stricken with infinity.
Then it drops, a blue rocket into the frigid
waters of Puget Sound.

Stricken too, I've dropped back
into place. We drift around the cove, never far
from the wooded shoreline. We're warned: *Hug the shore.*
Water this cold's fatal to a four-year-old.
Motherhood nips again—nothing

to explore in the limits of safety.
But our cove has revelations, the patient world:
on our slow paddle we taste ribbons of kelp–salty, bitter lettuce–
and blow hard bulbs like horns. The gravelled beach
slips from indigo to green,

sea urchins lilt on the tidal floor.
I lift Talia into my boat, show her how
the island's knobby ridge forms a beaked head. Flanks of fir
and redwood shape a winged creature who swooped
from her dark cave on the ocean floor.

Just Look

Meg

Fifth spring, as if a box opened, a polished child
stepped out: Talia's using words like
expectation, negotiation.
Plays some fancy word game,
shows us how to do the macarena. I watch her
pirouette in place where the old child stood.
Where did she learn that little whistle of esteem?
She knows everything now.

Once I explained how creeks and rivers begin
somewhere—
a little trickle of water, maybe a dark pool
hidden in a thicket where no creature larger than
a sparrow lives. Talia, her own beginning
a mystery, said, *Rivers just appear.*
And, *Rivers never end.*
I said, *There's always an end.*
Heavy rain came. She pointed to a backyard creek
risen suddenly from dry ground, a sinuous route
of murky water winding through tall grass.
And at the coast: *Just look.*
A small ravine dropped water thirty feet to the Pacific—
one grey channel, limitless to the horizon.

Sunday Hike at Point Reyes

Meg

    From the road we must be only slim pillars
    of color shifting along the ridge, wiped

    clean of identity. The late sun torches
    the clouds behind us and the afternoon

    seems empty of everything but silence.
    Sunday, the day of quiet urgency,

    never quite enough to make the long run
    of the week worth it. I feel our possibilities

    unravel when we do things like this,
    hiking a summer valley, copying

    our best experiences, believing somehow
    there could be a formula and enough practice.

Solomon's Child

—And the king said, Divide the living child in two.
I. Kings 3:27

Alice

I come home, Talia quivers with joy,
sensitive as a mimosa
to each appearance of the sun.

But a lesbian family has a Biblical lineage.
This little soft-fleshed animal,
her shining face so easily seduced
into love's service, divides herself daily
between mothers' arms.

And I—aren't all mothers covetous,
alert to intruders?—I want that face
for myself. Hourly I weigh my intentions:
this time, which of us must surrender her child?

Early Dawn Parallax

Meg

I wake so early the room seems
strange, too silent, colorless morning
leaking between blinds

like light of another world.
Alice's face half-buried, pale hair
swept across the pillow, body flattened,

just the curve of her buttocks
breaks a smooth line of covers. The cycle
of her breathing starts to pull me under,

but I enter a cramped, neglected
quarter of the mind. There—
there's the other life: July night

at the Little League, back in Mankota,
I'm in the bleachers rooting for the team.
I recognize faces—my children, friends,

the husband I didn't know I had.
At my cheek a cool breeze, humidity
of a different climate.

Urgent Care

Alice

In the pediatrician's office—
night hours and the waiting room full
of squalling babies—I wait with Meg,
Talia feverish in her arms.
Talia clutches my sleeve while Meg reads aloud,
one more *Berenstain Bears*.
We've had a long absence of touch.
The struggle to stop struggling—months now
we've been careful—all laid aside
in a panic over Talia's fever.
But there's a moment I look at Meg
instead of Talia, see again how unprotected she is.
I want to go home, drink some wine,
sink into bed. Maybe we'll find ourselves
kissing with relief, falling into
the sweet accident of skin on skin,
the gateway suddenly, urgently open.

IV — The Family Circle

Every trip by car Talia slumps in the back seat until she spots a Gap, a Borders, a factory outlet mall. Alice dreams of a jeep tour of the western states, but open spaces, empty highways hit Talia like carbon monoxide. Meg bargains for a hike, just a short walk together in the hills, but the pointlessness of it strikes Talia mute.

They go out for dinner. Alice chooses a little cafe, inventive and vegetarian, though Meg would prefer a good steak house. Talia of course wants pizza. Sunday morning Destiny's Child thumps upstairs on the stereo. Meg closes herself into the den with La Traviata. Alice escapes to the back yard, prunes the trumpet vine in search of silence.

So no one drinks alone in the garage half the night, no one's slammed against the bedroom wall—isn't the yoke of family life still impossible, differences stacking up, a tower of cracked plates? The same night they cook as a team, everyone happy with chicken cacciatore, or laugh together at the Marx Brothers, that night one of them dreams of being free.

The Laws of Planetary Motion

Talia

Look how they swing into orbit, circle like some weird planet's moons. Alice makes threats, doesn't listen. I scream refusals, then Meg's voice starts to rise—the closer Alice gets, the faster Meg moves in. Her daily path—she spins between us. I run to my room, slam the door, listen to the long silence. What pulls them? I'd be happy unbathed, feeding on pastry and gummy bears, staggering upstairs at midnight. Why be a boring fixed star, behave by the rules? I like to wear tank tops and shorts in December, show a few scribbled pages for homework, even if it starts them orbiting again.

This Way or That

Meg

    A shock, her chest budding at nine,
    dark springs of hair curling between her
    legs, beneath her arms. She snarls
    at me over breakfast, won't speak at dinner,
    throws her arms up, weeps
    if I say *Clean your room*. I study
    fitful clues: her tenth birthday, she decorates
    the house with Tweety Birds then puts
    Janet Jackson on the stereo
    and does a sexy lip-synch with her friends.

    At the mid-summer fair I watch her face
    spin by on a mechanical hang-glider.
    She soars in accelerating circles, ecstatic
    with flight. Rides the Zoomdive,
    the Kamikaze, anything with height, speed.
    We throw darts at tiny balloons, she
    wins the prize, selects a framed photo
    of a yellow kitten, I LOVE YOU printed
    in polka-dots across the bottom,
    then gives it to me.

    I read these changes like tea leaves:
    she'll be mercurial as Alice, need velocity
    in her life. No: her early sweetness will prevail.
    When the fireworks are over, we stroll
    from the fair by a small lagoon.
    Red, blue, orange lights of a huge Ferris wheel
    turn against the sky. Beside us
    another version: colored lights ripple
    on the surface of water.

Ten to Ten

Talia

1. Why am *I* sent to bed? Against my will. Most of my life against my will.

2. Tomorrow snow will fall. It will fall for me. In sheets of white, walls of lace. Will bury the brown grass, useless tomato vines. Curtain the houses around our house.

3. They're fighting next door. He always yells, she swears. Yuck, no, they're *doing it*. It's loud, must be funny they way they're laughing. They're really *doing it*.

4. Meg would say, *This is not a motel!*

5. California. It never snows. No sheets, no lace walls. I *hope* my parents never do it. Life—one long foggy day, too boring to believe.

6. In my Playmobil house they're whatever I want. There's a father. He's lying in the yard, his legs straight up. One mother. She's on the roof where I put her. A grandfather. He reads his stiff paper. I like their little fixed bodies.

7. Light goes out, room gets empty. Weird street noises, wailing. That boy down the block—stays up late, turns into a werewolf.

8. Kids in Africa sleep on straw beds. In Japan, little mats. Hawaii, probably hammocks. All around them palm trees, waves rolling, crashing. Yellow blossoms the size of lanterns at their heads.

9. Breakfast, Alice should have to make *cakes and honey*.

10. Dreams. Even asleep I'm awake. Dream wolves, dream snow, dream houses. Real dreams.

Eating at the In-laws

Alice

I know how skewed our life in California
looks here, but the dinner Meg's mother serves,
a dish of crusty chicken, breaded with crackers—
it swims in a canned-soup sauce.
There's salad: hacked iceberg, scraped carrots,
sliced radishes with bottled dressing.
A store-bought pie of flat pale cherries.

Meg's eyes meet mine. I think how I might
lay out arugula, oak leaf, tatsoi on a plate,
drizzle it with olive oil slightly green
in the cruet, sprinkle goat cheese,
some aged balsamic. I smile, stab a fork
into unhappy greens, let half
fall back to the bowl.

A weekend of croquet on the lawn,
pinochle after dinner, a backyard barbecue
for sixteen, I begin to settle in,
want to help with dinner.
Her mother hands me a head of lettuce, a knife.
I suddenly recall a salad I loved in my teens—
iceberg sliced into delicate strips,
a whole plateful, laced through
with coral ribbons of Kraft French.
Simple, sweet as a first infatuation,
it hooked me on food.

The chicken-fried steak she stirs
begins to seize me with hunger.
Her cousin's zucchini squares taste like custard,
soft with cheddar, long-cooked squash.
Garlic bread in oven-ready foil toasts up
to a crisp pungency. Betty Crocker brownies

still warm, a scoop of vanilla ice cream
trickling languorously down each side.

Now I can't wait for breakfast:
puffy French toast on sliced white bread:
it melts on the tongue.
And Mrs. Butterworth's Old-style
Real Blueberry Syrup.

The View from the North Coast

Meg

For twenty miles the shining ripple
of the Russian River's at our left.
Golden, green patchwork hills open to meadows
spinning with native grasses. Headlands
disappear abruptly at the slate-blue slick of the Pacific.
We've hit the coast, riding the wave
of Highway One to an almost silent world—
water, wind, chancy afternoon sun, fog rolling
at the western gate.

In the morning we rise early, stretch
in pale sun under a streaked sky.
Goldfinch flit between the cypress, harriers
scour the meadow, a clutch of wild turkeys
bob in the yard. Luxurious hours
I have, reading *A Wrinkle in Time* aloud with Talia,
making up wild stories of our own.

In the afternoon Talia and I
bring paper, watercolors to the beach
where, farther down, fat seals shine themselves
on rocks. Alice leans against a bleached log,
reads us a history of the coast: how the Pomo
lived here, survived with little but time for art,
communion. How they didn't work
unnecessary hours, didn't gather
more than they needed, never travelled
to an expensive but pristine place
to be uncomplicated again.

What We Told Ourselves

Alice

Doesn't matter. We should have gone back.

Stunned by the gruesome thunk, huge torso
in flight, hooves pedaling over the hood, car swerving
as if I'd released the wheel, we're speechless.
Then all at once: *God, a deer.*

I admit I think first of Talia in the back seat,
a child who broods for a squashed beetle,
a spider stranded in the toilet bowl.
I quickly lie. *It was instant, no suffering.*

Meg worries about the rented car, the damage
we've done. I pull over up the road, survey
a dented grill, dashed headlight. We hold off images
of a bleeding animal. Ask, *What could we do anyway?*

Wicked, how good we are
at making anything seem right.

In a night of little sleep, we hear scuttling
of some trapped creature for hours:
bird in the chimney, shrew in the walls, or worse,
a skunk. At breakfast Meg sighs,
Crazy, but all night I thought: the deer.

Yes. Now that it's pointless I'm certain.
We should've gone back.

At the Volcano

Alice

First weekend of the new year—
a friend and I on vacation,
our lovers left behind—we drive illegally
down a destroyed road
toward the erupting shelf of Kilauea.

At pavement's end we hike a mile by flashlight
over hardened *pahoehoe,*
ropes and glassy coils of cooled lava.
The polished bowl of Hawaiian sky
splinters with stars. Excitement rises between us,
palpable as reckless kisses.

Close up, the volcano's plume blazes against the sky,
blasts into sea. We can hardly breathe.
Then Maria whispers,
My God, the ground's glowing. Through cracks
in fragile rock a molten river runs, mere inches
beneath us. Our bodies turn molten too.
An agony of minutes, we spread out
for solid ground.

Afterward
we ride a wash of exhilaration for days,
survivors, not of catastrophe,
but of the free-fall into terror, the surface of disaster.
In our rapt communion, every illicit thing we do,
we understand the risk.

In Her Absence

Meg

These silent rooms evoke her speech
more clearly than actual conversation.
Movements I know so well—
how she sweeps through the door after work
to kiss Talia before bedtime,
her staccato chopping of onions, garlic
at the butcher block—
I feel them in my limbs.

I lift a shirt off a pile of laundry,
remind myself of her scent.
The unfinished glass of wine
among family photos, the odd book
left open, sorted mail piling up suggestively—
who is *this* from?—how inattentive I've been.

I'm keen for her to come home—but then
I'll lose her again. It's absence
that wakes me, brings me to my senses.

Return

Alice

I sank into the island's undertow.
Rain fell daily, yet light coaxed
its way through skies of violet, indigo.

All night hibiscus, plumeria leaked
the scent of seduction. Here, January—bleak
cold I'd bear easily if not for last week's

deliverance. Island life goes on. How
can that be, while I'm allowed
only winter? And fear: *Meg will find out.*

V — Perimenopausal Lovers Sleeping in Mid-winter

There's Meg flung out across the luxurious field of their bed, riding down dark hills of forgetfulness like a bear headed towards winter. Settled into a den of tissues and cough drops, water bottle and pills on the nightstand. Alice enters quietly, retrieves bedtime things, tiptoes downstairs to the guest room. She soon falls over the edge into a midnight landscape where all lost love is retrievable.

Meg gets up to the bathroom, so Alice stirs. Alice tosses in night sweats, Meg has chills. They've moved into a shared terrain so vast they don't recognize each other even as they meet. In the morning they'll only ask: How did you sleep? *Only answer,* Good, I feel better. *Never plumbing the blue song spinning through the open spaces of their life together.*

Late Season Mothers

Meg

At the water park the girls flee to the floating
rafts, preening, lily maids
on a turquoise pond. We're free to talk:
how their bodies changed this year. Amy's suit
rides high over newly-rounded cheeks,
Leila's peachy skin breaks out,
Talia's close to cleavage.
Mid-September, the heat's no longer sensuous
but old and tired, hills around us blond, dry.

I lie back, watch the earth slowly turn past
frayed clouds, a faded half-moon—
stars, planets lost behind that thick blue paint
of California sky. We pass each other lemonade,
plastic containers of sliced plums, melon.
Each privately studies her child,
feeling somehow wrong to be at menopause
with a daughter not yet started.

So we're old. The earth's old.
The shriek of girls volleys across the water:
wild whoops, primeval animals on the loose.

Star Quality

Talia

Thirteenth birthday, Meg's parents took me
to New York, *Miss Saigon*.
I told them how I wore purple velvet in our school play,
chose my part—Bloody Mary—
so I could walk as a queen in a blaze of spotlights.
Onstage my shyness disappeared,
the attention left me wired, almost fearless.

Meg fretted I'd forget my watch, my wallet,
my manners with her parents.
Alice worried my old homesickness would return.
(I bailed out of summer camp, sleepovers
were tricky for years.)
My only concern: what to wear to a matinee.

I know them. They counted the days, waited
for the phone all day. They've missed
their cue, don't see it's time—
scene's over: *totter on off stage.*

Kissing

Meg

I forgot kissing, the lingering kind—
not *Good Morning* or *Good-by*, not *I'm sorry*,
but what we did years ago: a first charged touch
lip to lip, then a tumble, a long clutching fall
into deep water, a well of a kiss, barely breathing.

One night, Talia in New York, we're on our
blue couch, *The French Lieutenant's Woman* on video.
The flushed intensity of Meryl Streep's skin,
her pale translucence, the soft luxury of her lips,
heated distance between him and her,
the movie one drawn-out, excruciating seduction.

Alice turns to me, close-focus, moves in,
halts. Our lips part, heads tilt—we're kissing.
Lights seem to dim. We kiss and kiss,
grateful for movies, each other again.

Hard Rain in San Francisco

Meg

After six dry months the first storm
stirs excitement. No one stays home.
Like snow in South Carolina, new rain
makes everyone forget how to drive:
see how they careen on drenched freeways.
Pedestrians slosh grey ribbons of sidewalk
into coffee shops, bookstores, pleased
with their boots and umbrellas.

But dreariness will set in soon.
Months of drizzle, fog sliding over the hills,
water pebbling down windows, sunshine
like an archaic memory. After every storm
trails through the hills are churned.

I worry about January and no beauty.
But you can live on tokens.
Walking to the market I find a sycamore leaf
broad as a globe, glistening at the edge
of a small puddle, continents etched
in olive, russet, mottled gold on its jagged face.
Without the patina of rain its colors
faded, its moment unseen forever.

Displeased

Meg

She left her hair all over the sink again, dark threads
curled into question marks around the drain.
I know they're not mine (short and grey).
But that's not what I hate or why I walk through her room
picking up clothes, retrieve a damp towel
left to moulder behind the door.

It's that she's sixteen, could pass for twenty,
and I feel her headed toward a world where she does
whatever she likes.
Her own sink, a bedroom
not at the end of my hall, a place I can't enter
when I need this maddening evidence of her.
And me, confined to phone calls, e-mail,
a minor player in her breakaway life.
She's just off to school this morning, likely thinking
(yet again), *Who could please her?*

It's true, she can't please me any more.
Right now my heart's like one of those tight balloons
deflating in one sharp gasp
as she swings out of the house.
She knows (I hope) there could never be
a child I'd love more, but today she can't please me.

She can't step into my arms to be lifted,
ride on my hip through the produce
naming fruits—*babana, appo*—
in that wispy high-pitched voice.
Or loll in my bed early morning, her wordless songs
like a determined bird experimenting in chilly air.
She won't ever call out at 3 a.m
half-whispering, half-shouting, *Mommie, Mommie, come.*

Insomnia

Alice

Now insomnia comes, a creditor
turning me out to the streets.
Stranded at 3 a.m. I hear
the distant screech of transit rails,
a lone bird trilling, the neighbor's
wretched dog. I tell myself
I can do without.
But I'm bereft. This street life
leads me to drugs—
Trazodone, Restoril.
I feel corrupted, decide
to go clean, but there's no denying
I've lost my claim
to the territory of youth.
I'm a transient now—no title
to anything but cold late hours,
contemplation of my colossal eviction.

Teenager on the Half-Shell

Talia

At sixteen, it's a revelation. Botticelli's
Venus, miraculously upright on the sea,
poised at the lip of a glittery shell:
goddess of love, she's shaped like me.

Soft-apple breasts, hips flagrantly wide,
belly a definite curve, a sweet shallow bowl—
her coy hands can't begin to hide
that sinuous flesh. A body I know—

barely narrowed waist, rounded thighs,
muscled calves, but I've never seen
its beauty—no match for the sleek girls, size
four, I contemplate in magazines.

Yet there I stand—tended, displayed:
newly born goddess, rocking the waves.

Exposure

Meg

She's about to go again. I smell it—
something tainted, smoky as a clump
of mushrooms, a decayed log.
Or the scent of burn, grinding her gears
on the precipice of despair.

I teach the same classes year after year,
hold onto the same friends.
Alice switches cafe to cafe—
urban migrant work, she calls it.
At a party I'm with friends while Alice
moves through the crowd, entices someone
to the back deck to smoke dope.
She's silent all day and I find her up
in the night—like *Jaws*, like shark music
playing in the background.
I wait, let the raw chill settle in.

When I was young I'd go outside early
to see if snow flattened
neighbor's flowers, smoothed lawns,
merged shrubbery, houses—
everything quiet against a faint mark of horizon.
The sky was exposed—like someone naked,
no one around. But it exposed me,
what it meant to be alone:
my voice couldn't pierce the empty space
between myself and the lit world of others' lives.

Another Black December

Alice

I listen: Talia's voice
down the hall, singing in her room
though wounded.
I sent her upstairs,
shrilled *prima donna* after her
because she didn't set the table.

The long march
through December, surviving on memory—
a season of irises dawning somewhere.
In my blue-black depths,
cold misery of dark months,
the beast of my father's wrath rises.
I wanted to grasp the soft flesh
of her arms, squeeze till my hands ached.

I keep thinking another woman
will get me through, take me to June,
soft air of the salt Atlantic coast
and that blitz of sun.

The third time I veered toward temptation
Meg said: *Go ahead.*
Learn what it's like out there,
where no one loves you like I do—
or did.

For the second time I don't tell her.

For the first time I know I'm not going anywhere.
But it rescues me, this dream—
remedy for the one where Meg walks out.

Winter Storm, Mendocino

Alice

Five days of rain, a steady beating
of water against the window.
Creeks north and south tip their banks.
We're closed in on the coast,
our borrowed home no longer a refuge.
High winds toss power lines,
leaving us to the chill dark, candles,
lantern, a small fire. A heavy cypress bough
sharpens itself on the roof all night.

Meg keeps to her chair by the fire,
turned away from everyone.

The final evening I hand Talia a jacket,
tell her we're going to town,
as if it's an adventure. But driving in the wet
black world I see Highway One dissolve
under headlights, and we slip blindly
into the night: nothing open, nothing lighted.
Unable to tell town from countryside
I've risked us in flight toward
something not out there.

A Sleep Genius

Meg

I turn over with confidence
in the middle of a quarrel,
drop like a plumb bob
to a watercolor of dreams.
I make sleep an ecstatic practice,
not only for dreams
or oblivion, that beautiful vacancy.
But in the temple of the bed,
fleeced blankets, fine cotton sheets,
body insensible, brain unfettered,
I hover out of sense, find narrow passages
into inner reaches, speechless spheres
waking practice tries to enter
through meditative sitting, eyes closed,
body stilled, in chaste imitation of divine sleep.

Evening Inversions

Alice

A lightning strike's been left to burn
in Illilouette gorge. Two fires are under watch
in Hetch Hetchy. Each night smoke drifts.

A scorched blanket settles over Yosemite.
Through tent canvas, we breathe fire-soot
all night. I dream I light cigarettes

after ten years' abstinence, our house ablaze.
Talia's eyes feel singed, Meg's nostrils sting,
morning toast tastes charred. Sun lifts the haze,

fresh air scours the valley—by day the sky reverts
to its shock of blue. Clean heat in the afternoon,
summer in the high country.

Back home: moods, silence.
Clear day masks damage here too, allows whatever
deception we choose.

But dirty evidence drops over us nightly—
I dream Meg's sleeping with
J.J., my old girlfriend, the one she hates.

Their bodies melt like wax under flame, fuse
into my perfect lover. That's how I
get through the night.

Damage

Meg

I dream I travel the western states
setting wildfires. Sling lit cigarettes out the window,
drop flaming letters in national parks,
buy a butane lighter and head to the Sierra.
Always it's a shock, something I drive away from
in horror. How does it keep happening?
People read of my work: the Bitterroots to the San Gabriels,
Cascades to the Tetons, forests blaze.

Back home friends trade litanies of loss:
lovers leaving, kids on drugs. I'm the lucky one,
life on the road, nothing to fear but
the *boom-vroom* of thunder, strobe-flashes of lightning.
I dine on barbecue, submerge myself
in motels' blue water. I know what it means
to be tender meat tossed on hot coals.
But after damage one heals.

Later I backtrack, see green saplings,
pink spikes of fireweed poking through powdery ashes.
I study charred terrain so leafy the teetering height
of blackened skeletons doesn't matter.

Next season: another chance to find revelation.
A *real* burning bush, one more living thing
not willing to be consumed.

After We Fight

Meg

    I walk the long route around
    the neighborhood. Something lustrous,
    dark and metallic, swoops by—
    large wings, wedged tail: a raven.
    It settles on a scraggly cedar, a lone bird—
    though ravens travel together, pair up
    for life. I watch it loop, almost somersault
    toward the north, flutter and turn east.
    There, a second bird hovers.
    Why that distance? Does she long to leave him
    in the tree, does he crave not to follow—
    and their wiring won't let go? Are there days
    they can't stand the sound
    of each other's flapping?

    Alice and I—we're yoked that way.
    Mostly instinct, little choice?
    An hour ago I thought of leaving, but I jog back,
    revise the bird story: they glided
    wing-to-wing all morning, one leading,
    the other taking over. Drift apart now
    to find that urge again. Soon they'll head out,
    scout a ripe carcass, pick it loose, pull
    steamy tidbits up, dangle them for one another.
    Even in their distance they may be calling
    back and forth. Love-croaks,
    so low I can't hear them.

Vll — The Afternoon Nap

Alice leaves the hospital, her mother anchored with tubes. Days of anxious attendance, now a few hours to be beyond reach. What does she do with freedom? Drives down Calhoun Street, turns in at the retirement home. Upstairs her mother's sofa, the long green and white weave of it, waits. Slight imprint of her mother's head on the pillow, it draws her in—

She closes her eyes. The world still touches her: infusion of sunlight on her cheek, languid air filtering in from the balcony. Cushions that exhale her mother's scent. A last chance to receive whatever lingers in that white room on the fourth floor. A last chance to lie with her mother, no worry about flesh on flesh, mother and daughter.

Beatitude

Alice

It's like being with Talia as a baby again,
a rivulet of milky oatmeal down your chin
I catch and slip back in.
You're so tired, too tired for food.
The corner of your mouth, not quite closed,
no longer moves.
How slowly the body shuts down.

Working hard together, we spend two hours
on a little warm cereal, a few pieces of orange, some tea.

You were patient like that when I was a child,
weak with flu. You sat on my bed,
scraped at an apple with a sharp spoon, as long
as necessary. You put it to my lips,
its texture tingly, pulpy on my tongue.
When I was well I begged for more,
wanting the apple and your time.

With Talia it was little jars of pears.
We'd had her five months, still learning
each other's ways. At the zoo she sat on my lap,
eyed caged monkeys feeding in their courtyard,
Tropical trees shimmied in the breeze.
The siamangs trumpeted wildly
and she began to wail.

I paced the sidewalk, showed her
trees in motion. She began to settle in,
waving her arms like the monkeys,
chattering, screeching, then quiet as I scooped
dribbles of pear from her chin, tipped them in.

A sense of blessedness fell upon us—

the short rain tempered by sun, bougainvillea
flaring on the chain fences.

From her I learned about the body,
how not to be repelled by colorful excretions—
the smelly brown diaper, milky spit-up on the shoulder,
little candlesticks of green below her nose.

After the ordeal of breakfast I get you to the toilet,
wipe your backside (routinely now), settle you
in bed, then leave as you begin to nap,
closer to dying than I know.

It's Her Body I Miss Now

Alice

1.
My mother so private, hiding her body's changes—
hollowed chest, zippered scars—
like a child who'd done a bad thing.
In the end she surrendered and I washed her flesh, fine porcelain,
as if she weren't my mother.

Afterward we talked as before. I stroked her hand: her skin
always silky, could not bear a label
at her neckline, an unfinished seam.
Needles, tapes, tubes marked it blue-black, purple:
a chain of storm clouds looming on each arm.

One afternoon, a dark September,
rain outside, I sat at her bed, my arm beside hers,
saw what I haven't seen for years:
how young I still am.
I saw what my mother needed—to be gathered up, held.
I crept into the barred bed, curled around her
in that metal crib, cradled her in sleep.

2.
Five nights after her death she appears in a dream.
I'm frightened.
We don't speak but I touch her arm: warm, real as ever.

Every time I returned to South Carolina we talked,
things never said before.
But only through her body I find her, the way
we first knew each other.

Not Easy to Know

Alice

I want my brother to feel the pull of my memories:
Mother counting out French numbers with me in the bathtub,
singing "Mockingbird Hill" in her thin off-key voice,
making the same yellow sundress for each of us.

Can he love these memories too?
Will they lighten his grief or burden him more?

We're walking at night through Charleston streets
where even the stars seem like onyx. He says little.
It's not easy to know what he feels. But he takes my hand,
never changes the subject on our way back home.

Edisto Island

Alice

In the afternoon things are still.
The ocean breeze dies out, a thick haze
of heat across the dunes.
After the funeral we keep to the house,
drink wine on the veranda, then eat late—
fresh shrimp dropped in a pan
skimmed with butter.

We speak of my mother, how she
loved this island. Aunt Louisa's
usually in bed by nine, but tonight she won't
stop talking: *Your mother had a lover for years,
all that time.* Like me, she tells everything.

My brother slips off to bed. My cousin
picks ups a book. Louisa and I go on half the night.
Mother seemed to know nothing of love.
At three a.m. I fall asleep, my mother a stranger,
gone farther away than ever.

Dead Center

Alice

In the half-lit rooms of the afterlife
my father carries on as usual. He slaps the table,
shouts *Hell, no*. No one knows
what he's talking about. My mother ignores him.
She rides an exercise bike and sings Cole Porter.
Grandmother arranges roses and preaches.
Aunt Rudy stretches on the bed, calls for someone
to talk to. Aunt Aggie cans peaches in the kitchen.
The uncles sit together, hearing aids turned off.

They try to stay occupied, otherwise things get
too dead. Sometimes they gather
at the table, pour a few drinks and joke around.
The party goes on for days, like one of their wakes.
I hear them in the distance.
Then I have to touch someone—
Meg, Talia. I have to say something out loud.

Vll — From the Backyard at Nine P. M.

A sharp angle of streetlight on the kitchen door, an unfamiliar cat's shadow hunched beside it—Alice looks on from the dark, thinks it could be someone else's house. Inside, a woman's framed by the French doors. But Alice knows her, the length of her body, its most intimate movements. And the way she stands impatient at the sink while the water runs hot, slaps the dishtowel back on its hook. Knows she turns Cecilia Bartoly up full blast when no one's home, spends hours on a watercolor of one lopsided eggplant.

It's a long time since Alice first saw her, a dark-haired girl with a fistful of friends. A long time since she tried to pry her loose from her friends. In that alien kitchen the woman's silver hair's darkened by dim light and she's a stranger again, laughing on the phone with someone Alice still wishes she didn't know.

Out of the Ordinary

Alice

I lock the door, leave behind
a clean kitchen, laundry full of food-stained clothes.
Drive off to Anza-Borrego, a place
solitary as a stone, mile after mile of rough road,
beer cans, broken bottles.

What do I find?
Barrel cactus, saguaro, echinopsis.
At the pock-marked carcass of an old truck, I see
a good set of ruts, drive halfway down the canyon,
start to worry about weather, a cloudburst
flushing through, the road washing out.

I give up, park, walk around under that sky,
the car in sight—landscape
like an endless mirror.

Ocotillos have erupted, brittle brown Medusae,
ten foot stalks bare until the right rain,
right temperature lets them sprout.
Their thorny spikes are strung with green ears, trumpets
of red light. They shift shape at every angle,
seem to wave without motion.

So many, they look ordinary.
In this strange place, my life extraordinary,
even to me.

Painted Moon, Painted Valley

Alice

I hate to leave, can't bear how their sweet
adhesive love takes off my skin at good-by,
but all I want is to drive this silver-streaked
road, green and yellow valley, all day, all night.

Lose ordinary time on an unknown route,
anywhere distant, just some miles to be alone.
The windows down, wind whipping through
like a storm, dry gusts of a slot canyon.

See the sun flare out, a last swipe of gold,
the moon rise full, almost pink in the violet air—
now it's one of Meg's watercolors. At my core
taut fibers start to give: I'm there, already there.

It just takes a painted moon, painted valley,
a strange road north to get where I want to be.

Appetite

Talia

Every part of me is hungry, every cell
a small animal kicking away on its wheel.
My arms, legs tremble, my skin ticks with hunger.
I feed this humger: red meat, fresh bread, chocolate
and fancy cream. It smacks its lips
and yells for more. I starve it: it collapses
into something mean, a snake coiled in my belly.
I'm in the streets mid-afternoon, needing
to be seen, scanning faces for recognition—
of what? What? I snap at everyone I know,
want a life with new people, can't be happy
with anything. Nighttime, it hijacks my dreams,
sweeps me down dark avenues where I'm mixed up
with strangers who abandon me at dawn.
Hunger's like a child, whining, insatiable—
what's it whimpering about now? No one knows.
But desire lines my mouth, my throat's wet
with it, my heart jerks in its cage, desolate.
When I was a child, I took off on my bicycle,
rode on craving. I saved myself from city streets,
made it to somewhere green, green enough
that time and hunger stalled. I held on, sure
I'd be filled some day. Now I know: my body's
a forever-hungry thing. Female, no cure in this life.

Lost Cause

Meg

Lit up, urgent to be out in the world,
Talia rides BART to the East Bay,
hangs out in Berkeley. Or Muni downtown,
South of Market on the weekends.
Goes with friends or by herself, just goes.
Never brings anyone over. Is it because
we're lesbian? Perfect irony—
I've forgotten how to be a lover, know only
how to be a mother. Like someone
who hears herself referred to as a famous diva
after she's lost the voice.

Once in Precita Park I watched Talia
tell a little friend a pointless story.
She labored so I saw she loved her friend
a degree too much. The worst of it—
sometimes it's the mother's job to do nothing.
You'd move fast, unseen as a lion
through tall grass, to save your child,
but no, you have to pace inside yourself,
count your own wounds for distraction.
Then start over, do it again.

Four A. M. at the Open Window

Alice

Streetlight dapples the Chinese elms, tiny bright
birds shivering on upper branches. White anemones,

hollyhock give back light from the night garden.
The summer air's so still, hollowness of space

almost audible. I realize not much
secures me here. Not gravity. Just the slight motion

of breathing, the little in and out at the nostrils.
Minus that, I'd spin loose, fade across empty reaches.

What woke me? An interior voice needing
to touch on mortality at a time I'd listen.

Cutting Edge

Alice

J.J. comes through town. We drink wine,
talk about that spring in Death Valley.
I made her camp in the cindered landscape
of Ubehebe crater— *to loosen ties to the ordinary world.*
God, a freezing night, gripping each other,
tracking the howls of some grisly creature
who circled us till dawn.
    I sound crazy.

Roxie sends old photos, notes on the back.
In one we lean together against a blue fir, high
in the Selkirks, the two of us for weeks.
    I barely remember.
My thirtieth birthday, cycling Orcas Island,
a paceline of women. We caught a tailwind
downhill to the water.
    In the blurred shot I look wild with speed.

All I want is to be at home, please Meg somehow,
cook with Talia: last night we simmered a mole sauce,
ground up chocolate, chipotles.
    Meg says I'm not so edgy any more.
Yes. I've lost my edge—nothing but a sharp thing inside
that kept me moving.

Unseasoned

Meg

It's the absence of autumn in San Francisco
that's deceived me: nothing flares on the horizon
to warn of coming chill. Or it's how spring

hovers, descends any time: azaleas fall open
in November, the mercury settles at 60 mid-winter,
and in July, fog filters out the heat. Maybe it's

the fog: all that silver light suggests suffering's
unnecessary. Years disappear, blown off
in a soft breeze—no thunder of the real about it—

fifty years, but I'm still lured in: maybe aging
won't be so bad. I must need heat souring everything
like old wine, everyone uncorked by August,

and those stiff Minnesota winters, to know
the end comes on and on. I'm going gracefully,
just curious: how cold is the cold, if cold is all that waits?

Exposure

Meg

So Alice loves me now. Watches like I'm a rare bird
loose from its cage. She cooks jambalaya,
lamb ragu, lavish stews of remorse. Though why-did-she-
want-me? still wounds like that splinter of bone
hidden in the hot curry. Did she need a guiltless girl?
Someone to plead her troubled case with the world.

But year after year I shut the door of my studio,
put on a headset, painted half the night.
For Talia I'd be the two a.m. savior
from nightmares at a friend's house, faithful
homework partner though hopeless in higher math.
Of course I wanted Talia for myself.
Nights Alice came weeping—such a knack
for repentence—I held out. (Only my arms weakened,
pulled her close again.) I know I left her.
Even when her mother died, she didn't protest.

If she's truly spent her discontent, how do I
wean myself from loving the cold?
Hers are purer transgressions. She deserves heat, sun,
balm of some summery redemption.

A New Period of Red

Meg

    I watch her loosen the gauzy ribbon,
    open the box, lift out a crimson camisole
    and slinky scanties, laugh.
    But she takes the bait, arches her spine,
    tucks her legs under like a model in a lingerie catalog—
    where I did *not* order this gift.
    I found it innocently, next to flannel nightgowns
    at Nordstrom's. I stroked the satin,
    felt compelled to lift it, run my hand beneath
    its folds. Imagined her—
    scarlet woman of a certain age.
    And for myself a ruby-colored mini-slip, bikini briefs.
    Through with the red stain on the sheet,
    we'll turn to red satin.

Old Sweethearts

Alice

Beads of light spill through blinds
on your bare shoulder. Your face
is aging into softness, innocent
on the pillow. I still feel some heat, relief
of your touch. We've moved closer again
in sleep. Yesterday we walked the hills, spring
starting to open wild iris, lupine. I bought
red gladioli, a vase of flaming tongues.

We'll stay home tonight—you and I.
I'm surprised how I thrived after all,
survived family life like a woodland creature
who prospers in the sun: caught the art
of staying cool, going for days on one deep drink.
And all this time you've shed layers: a madrone,
tawny strips curling off, down to the quick,
satiny limbs. Luxurious to touch and sweet to burn.

Books Available from Gival Press

A Change of Heart by David Garrett Izzo
    1st edition, ISBN 1-928589-18-9, $20.00

    A historical novel about Aldous Huxley and his circle "astonishingly alive and accurate."
    — Roger Lathbury, George Mason University

Barnyard Buddies I by Pamela Brown; illustrations by Annie H. Hutchins
    1st edition, ISBN 1-928589-15-4, $16.00

    Thirteen stories filled with a cast of creative creatures both engaging and educational. "These stories in this series are delightful. They are wise little fables, and I found them fabulous."
    — Robert Morgan, author of *This Rock* and *Gap Creek*

Barnyard Buddies II by Pamela Brown; illustrations by Annie H. Hutchins
    1st edition, ISBN 1-928589-21-9, $16.00

    "Children's literature which emphasizes good character development is a welcome addition to educators' as well as parents' resources."
    — Susan McCravy, elementary school teacher

Bones Washed With Wine: Flint Shards from Sussex and Bliss by Jeff Mann
    1st edition, ISBN 1-928589-14-6, $15.00

    A special collection of lyric intensity, including the 1999 Gival Press Poetry Award winning collection. Jeff Mann is "a poet to treasure both for the wealth of his language and the generosity of his spirit."
    — Edward Falco, author of *Acid*

Canciones para sola cuerda / Songs for a Single String by Jesús Gardea; English translation by Robert L. Giron
    1st edition, ISBN 1-928589-09-X, $15.00

    A moving collection of love poems, with echoes of *Neruda à la Mexicana* as Gardea writes about the primeval quest for the perfect woman. "The free verse...evokes the quality and forms of cante hondo, emphasizing the emotional interplay of human voice and guitar."
    — Elizabeth Huergo, Montgomery College

Dead Time / Tiempo muerto by Carlos Rubio
    1st edition, ISBN 1-928589-17-0, $21.00

    This bilingual (English/Spanish) novel is "an unusual tale of love, hate, passion and revenge."
    — Karen Sealy, author of *The Eighth House*

Dervish by Gerard Wozek
> 1st edition, ISBN 1-928589-11-1, $15.00
>
> Winner of the 2000 Gival Press Poetry Award. This rich whirl of the dervish traverses a grand expanse from bars to crazy dreams to fruition of desire. "By Jove, these poems shimmer."
> — Gerry Gomez Pearlberg, author of *Mr. Bluebird*

Dreams and Other Ailments / Sueños y otros achaques by Teresa Bevin
> 1st edition, ISBN 1-928589-13-8, $21.00
>
> Winner of the Bronze Award – 2001 *ForeWord Magazine's* Book of the Year Award for Translation. A wonderful array of short stories about the fantasy of life and tragedy but filled with humor and hope. "*Dreams and Other Ailments* will lift your spirits."
> — Lynne Greeley, The University of Vermont

The Gay Herman Melville Reader by Ken Schellenberg
> 1st edition, ISBN 1-928589-19-7, $16.00
>
> A superb selection of Melville's work. "Here in one anthology are the selections from which a serious argument can be made by both readers and scholars that a subtext exists that can be seen as homoerotic."
> — David Garrett Izzo, author of *Christopher Isherwood: His Era, His Gang, and the Legacy of the Truly Strong Man*

Let Orpheus Take Your Hand by George Klawitter
> 1st edition, ISBN 1-928589-16-2, $15.00
>
> Winner of the 2001 Gival Press Poetry Award. A thought provoking work that mixes the spiritual with stealthy desire, with Orpheus leading us out of the pit. "These poems present deliciously sly metaphors of the erotic life that keep one reading on, and chuckling with pleasure."
> — Edward Field, author of *Stand Up, Friend, With Me*

Literatures of the African Diaspora by Yemi D. Ogunyemi
> 1st edition, ISBN 1-928589-22-7, $20.00
>
> An important study of the influences in literatures of the world. "It, indeed, proves that African literatures are, without mincing words, a fountainhead of literary divergence."
> —Joshua 'Kunle Awosan, University of Massachusetts Dartmouth.

Metamorphosis of the Serpent God by Robert L. Giron
> 1st edition, ISBN 1-928589-07-3, $12.00
>
> "Robert Giron's biographical poetry embraces the past and the present, ethnic and sexual identity, themes both mythical and personal."
> — *The Midwest Book Review*

Middlebrow Annoyances: American Drama in the 21st Century by Myles Weber
> 1st edition, ISBN 1-928589-20-0, $20.00
>
> "Weber's intelligence and integrity are unsurpassed by anyone writing about the American theatre today..."
> — John W. Crowley, The University of Alabama at Tuscaloosa

The Nature Sonnets by Jill Williams
> 1st edition, ISBN 1-928589-10-3, $8.95
>
> An innovative collection of sonnets that speaks to the cycle of nature and life, crafted with wit and clarity. "Refreshing and pleasing."
> — Miles David Moore, author of *The Bears of Paris*

Prosody in England and Elsewhere: A Comparative Approach by Leonardo Malcovati
> 1st edition, ISBN 1-928589-26-X, $16.00
>
> "To write about the structure of poetry for a non-specialist audience takes a brave author. To do so in a way that is readable, in fact enjoyable, without sacrificing scholarly standards takes an accomplished author."
> —Frank Anshen, State University of New York

The Smoke Week: Sept. 11-21, 2001 by Ellis Avery
> 1st edition, ISBN 1-928589-24-3, $15.00
>
> *Writer's Notes Magazine* 2004 Book Award—Notable for Culture.
> Winner of the Ohioana Library Walter Rumsey Marvin Award
> "Here is Witness. Here is Testimony."
> — Maxine Hong Kingston, author of *The Fifth Book of Peace*

Songs for the Spirit by Robert L. Giron
> 1st edition, ISBN 1-928589-08-1, $16.95
>
> This humanist psalter reflects a vision of the new millennium, one that speaks to readers regardless of their spiritual inclination. "This is an extraordinary book."
> — John Shelby Spong, author of *Why Christianity Must Change or Die: A Bishop Speaks to Believers in Exile*

Sweet to Burn by Beverly Burch
> 1st edition, ISBN 1-928589-23-5, $15.00
>
> Winner of the 2003 Gival Press Poetry Award
> "Novelistic in scope, but packing the emotional intensity of lyric poetry..."
> — Eloise Klein Healy, author of *Passing*

Tickets to a Closing Play by Janet I. Buck
    1st edition, ISBN 1-928589-25-1, $15.00

    Winner of the 2002 Gival Press Poetry Award
    "...this rich and vibrant collection of poetry [is] not only serious and insightful, but a sheer delight to read."
    — Jane Butkin Roth, editor, *We Used to Be Wives: Divorce Unveiled Through Poetry*

Wrestling with Wood by Robert L. Giron
    3rd edition, ISBN 1-928589-05-7, $5.95

    A chapbook of impressionist moods and feelings of a long-term relationship which ended in a tragic death. "Nuggets of truth and beauty sprout within our souls."
    — Teresa Bevin, author of *Havana Split*

For Book Orders Only, Call: 877.727.5764
Or Write : Gival Press, LLC / PO Box 3812 / Arlington, VA 22203
Visit: www.givalpress.com

www.ingramcontent.com/pod-product-compliance
Lightning Source LLC
Chambersburg PA
CBHW031204090426
42736CB00009B/776